ADHD in the Workplace

Navigating Success - Strategies for Productivity and Harmony

Alex Hartley

This document is geared towards providing exact and reliable information with regards to the topic and issue covered. The publication is sold with the idea that the publisher is not required to render accounting, officially permitted, or otherwise, qualified services. If advice is necessary, legal or professional, a practiced individual in the profession should be ordered.

From a Declaration of Principles which was accepted and approved equally by a Committee of the American Bar Association and a Committee of Publishers and Associations.

The information herein is offered for informational purposes solely, and is universal as so. The presentation of the information is without contract or any type of guarantee assurance.

The trademarks that are used are without any consent, and the publication of the trademark is without permission or backing by the trademark owner. All trademarks and brands within this book are for clarifying purposes only and are owned by the owners themselves, not affiliated with this document.

TABLE OF CONTENTS

Chapter 1: Understanding ADHD and Its Impact

Introduction

Imagine a world where your mind is a vibrant kaleidoscope of thoughts, ideas, and impulses, constantly shifting and swirling in a dazzling array of colors and patterns. This is the reality for many individuals living with Attention Deficit Hyperactivity Disorder (ADHD). While the experience can be exhilarating and creative, it can also present unique challenges in daily life. In this chapter, we'll explore the intricacies of ADHD and provide practical strategies to help you thrive on this remarkable journey.

Understanding the ADHD Brain

Before we dive into the practical aspects, let's take a moment to appreciate the unique wiring of the ADHD brain. Contrary to popular belief, ADHD is not a deficit or a disorder; it's a neurological difference that shapes how your brain processes information and regulates attention.

Imagine your brain as a busy city, with neurons firing like traffic signals, directing the flow of information and impulses. In the ADHD brain, some of these signals might get a little crossed or delayed, leading to a unique experience of the world around you.

- You might find yourself hyperfocused on a task that captivates your interest, losing track of time and ignoring external distractions.
- On the other hand, mundane or repetitive tasks might feel like an uphill battle, as your brain seeks constant stimulation and novelty.
- You might find yourself interrupting conversations or blurting out thoughts before processing them fully, a manifestation of impulsivity.

These experiences are not flaws; they are simply the way your brain is wired, and understanding this can help you embrace your neurodiversity with pride.

Strategies for Thriving with ADHD

While ADHD presents its own set of challenges, there are numerous strategies and techniques you can employ to harness your strengths and overcome obstacles. Here are some practical tips to help you navigate your journey:

1. Embrace Your Strengths

ADHD is often associated with incredible creativity, innovative thinking, and the ability to see things from unique perspectives. Embrace these strengths and find ways to incorporate them into your daily life and pursuits.

- Pursue hobbies or careers that allow you to channel your creativity and hyperfocus abilities.

- Surround yourself with like-minded individuals who appreciate your unique way of thinking.
- Don't be afraid to think outside the box and challenge conventional wisdom.

2. Create a Supportive Environment

Your environment can either hinder or facilitate your ability to manage ADHD symptoms. Take control by making simple adjustments that cater to your needs:

- Minimize distractions in your workspace by decluttering and creating a dedicated study or work area.
- Use color-coding, labels, or visual cues to help you stay organized and on track.
- Incorporate physical movement into your routine, such as taking breaks for short walks or incorporating a standing desk.

3. Develop Time Management Strategies

Time management can be a significant challenge for individuals with ADHD, but with the right strategies, it can become a manageable skill:

- Break larger tasks into smaller, more manageable steps and set achievable goals.
- Use timers or alarms to stay focused and prevent hyperfocus on a single task.
- Prioritize tasks and learn to say "no" when overwhelmed, avoiding burnout.

4. Build a Support System

Living with ADHD can be a rollercoaster ride, and it's essential to have a strong support system to help you navigate the ups and downs:

- Surround yourself with understanding friends, family members, or colleagues who can provide encouragement and accountability.

- Join online communities or support groups to connect with others who share similar experiences.
- Consider working with a therapist or coach who specializes in ADHD, providing you with personalized strategies and guidance.

5. Practice Self-Care and Mindfulness

Taking care of your physical and mental well-being is crucial for managing ADHD symptoms and reducing stress levels:

- Incorporate regular exercise into your routine, as physical activity can help improve focus and concentration.
- Practice mindfulness techniques, such as meditation or deep breathing exercises, to calm your mind and improve emotional regulation.
- Prioritize self-care activities that bring you joy and relaxation, whether it's reading,

listening to music, or spending time in nature.

Conclusion

Navigating the ADHD journey is a unique and rewarding experience. By embracing your strengths, creating a supportive environment, developing time management strategies, building a support system, and prioritizing self-care, you can unlock your full potential and thrive in all aspects of your life. Remember, ADHD is not a limitation; it's a unique way of experiencing the world, and with the right tools and mindset, you can turn it into a superpower.

What is ADHD?

Attention Deficit Hyperactivity Disorder (ADHD) is a neurological condition that affects the way an individual's brain processes information, regulates attention, and manages impulses and hyperactivity. Despite being a widely recognized disorder, ADHD is often misunderstood, and misconceptions about its nature and impact can lead to stigma and challenges for those living with it.

ADHD is characterized by three primary symptom categories: inattention, hyperactivity, and impulsivity. These symptoms can manifest in various ways, depending on the individual and the situation.

Inattention

- Difficulty sustaining focus and attention on tasks or activities
- Easily distracted by external stimuli
- Tendency to be forgetful and disorganized
- Struggles with following instructions or completing tasks

Hyperactivity

- Excessive physical movement, fidgeting, or restlessness
- Difficulty remaining still or quiet for extended periods
- Tendency to talk excessively or interrupt others

Impulsivity

- Acting without considering consequences
- Difficulty waiting their turn or delaying gratification
- Blurting out responses or interrupting others

It's important to note that not all individuals with ADHD exhibit all three symptom categories, and the severity of symptoms can vary significantly from person to person.

ADHD is not a disorder that is outgrown; it is a lifelong condition that can have a profound impact on various aspects of an individual's life, including academic performance, social relationships, and professional endeavors. However, with proper diagnosis, treatment, and support strategies, individuals with ADHD can manage their symptoms and lead successful and fulfilling lives.

Diagnosis of ADHD typically involves a comprehensive evaluation by a licensed healthcare professional, such as a psychologist, psychiatrist, or pediatrician. The evaluation may include interviews, behavioral assessments, rating scales, and ruling out other potential underlying conditions.

Treatment for ADHD often involves a combination of approaches, including medication, behavioral therapy, educational interventions, and lifestyle modifications. Stimulant medications, such as methylphenidate (Ritalin) and amphetamines (Adderall), are commonly prescribed to help improve focus, impulse control, and reduce hyperactivity. However, medication alone is not a cure-all, and it is often combined with other interventions tailored to the individual's needs.

By understanding ADHD as a neurological condition and providing the necessary support and accommodations, individuals with ADHD can overcome challenges, capitalize on their strengths, and achieve their full potential in all areas of life.

Common Challenges in the Workplace

For individuals with Attention Deficit Hyperactivity Disorder (ADHD), the workplace can present a unique set of challenges that can impact their productivity, performance, and overall well-being. Here are some common challenges that individuals with ADHD may encounter in the workplace:

1. **Time Management and Prioritization**
    - Difficulty managing time effectively, leading to missed deadlines or last-minute rushes
    - Struggling to prioritize tasks and allocate time appropriately
    - Challenges with planning and organizing work efficiently
2. **Attention and Focus**

- Easily distracted by external stimuli or internal thoughts
- Difficulty sustaining attention on tasks, especially those that are repetitive or mundane
- Challenges with multitasking or switching between tasks seamlessly

3. **Hyperactivity and Restlessness**
    - Feeling restless or fidgety during meetings or prolonged periods of sitting
    - Difficulty remaining still or quiet, which can be disruptive in certain work environments
    - Tendency to interrupt others or speak out of turn due to impulsivity

4. **Memory and Organization**

- Struggles with remembering instructions, appointments, or details
- Difficulty maintaining an organized workspace or keeping track of important documents
- Challenges with following through on tasks or completing projects from start to finish

5. **Emotional Regulation**

- Experiencing emotional outbursts or mood swings due to impulsivity or sensitivity
- Difficulty managing frustration or stress in challenging work situations
- Struggles with interpersonal relationships or conflict resolution

•

6. **Procrastination and Motivation** Tendency to procrastinate or become distracted by more interesting or stimulating tasks

- Challenges with initiating and sustaining effort on tasks that are perceived as boring or mundane
- Difficulty maintaining motivation over extended periods of time

While these challenges can be significant, it is important to recognize that individuals with ADHD possess unique strengths and abilities that can be valuable assets in the workplace. With the right support, accommodations, and strategies, they can overcome these challenges and thrive in their professional endeavors.

Employers can play a crucial role in creating an inclusive and supportive environment by providing reasonable accommodations, encouraging open communication, and fostering a culture of understanding and acceptance for neurodiversity in the workplace.

Strengths and Unique Perspectives

While Attention Deficit Hyperactivity Disorder (ADHD) presents certain challenges, it is essential to recognize the remarkable strengths and unique perspectives that individuals with ADHD possess. These qualities, when harnessed and nurtured, can be powerful assets in various aspects of life, including the workplace, relationships, and personal growth.

1. **Creativity and Innovation**

    - Individuals with ADHD often possess a remarkable ability to

-

  think outside the box and approach problems from unique angles.

  Their divergent thinking and ability to make unexpected connections can lead to innovative solutions and groundbreaking ideas.

- This creativity can be invaluable in fields such as art, design, entrepreneurship, and problemsolving.

2. **Hyperfocus and Passion**

   - When engaged in tasks or activities that captivate their interest, individuals with ADHD can experience a state of intense focus and concentration known as hyperfocus.

- This hyperfocus can lead to remarkable productivity, attention to detail, and a deep level of immersion in the task at hand.

-

   Harnessing this ability can be advantageous in fields that require sustained focus, such as research, coding, or creative pursuits.

3. **Adaptability and Resilience**

- Individuals with ADHD often develop a remarkable ability to adapt to changing circumstances and bounce back from setbacks.
- Their flexible thinking and resourcefulness can be assets in dynamic environments or situations that require quick pivots and problem-solving.
- This resilience can also foster a growth mindset and a willingness to embrace challenges as opportunities for personal development.

4. **High Energy and Enthusiasm**

Many individuals with ADHD possess a boundless energy and enthusiasm that can be contagious and inspiring to those around them.

- This energy can be channeled into projects, initiatives, or team environments, fueling motivation and driving progress.
- Their passion and excitement can also contribute to a positive and dynamic work culture.

5. **Multitasking and Quick Thinking •**

While multitasking can be a double-edged sword, some individuals with ADHD possess a remarkable ability to juggle multiple tasks or rapidly switch between them.

-

- Their quick thinking and ability to process information quickly can be valuable in fast-paced environments or situations that require quick decision-making.
- This skill can be particularly useful in fields such as crisis management, emergency response, or high-pressure sales.

It is essential to recognize and celebrate the unique strengths and perspectives that individuals with ADHD bring to the table. By creating an environment that embraces neurodiversity and provides the necessary support and accommodations, organizations and communities can benefit from the incredible talents and contributions of individuals with ADHD.

Chapter 2: Building SelfAwareness and Self-Acceptance

Building Self-Awareness and SelfAcceptance for Individuals with ADHD

Living with Attention Deficit Hyperactivity Disorder (ADHD) can be a journey filled with challenges and triumphs. Along this path, developing self-awareness and cultivating self-acceptance are crucial steps towards thriving and embracing one's unique strengths and abilities. Here are some strategies for building self-awareness and self-acceptance for individuals with ADHD:

1. **Understand Your Neurodiversity**

   - Recognize that ADHD is a neurological condition, not a personal flaw or shortcoming.
   - Learn about the science behind ADHD and how it affects

cognitive processes, emotions, and behaviors.

- Embrace your neurodiversity as a unique way of experiencing and interacting with the world.

2. **Identify Your Strengths and Talents •** Take time to reflect on your natural abilities, interests, and the areas where you excel.

    - Celebrate your creativity, problem-solving skills, resilience, and ability to think outside the box.
    - Focus on developing and leveraging these strengths in various aspects of your life.

3. **Practice Self-Compassion**

    - Be kind and patient with yourself, recognizing that ADHD presents unique challenges.

- Avoid self-criticism or harsh selfjudgment when facing difficulties or setbacks.
- Treat yourself with the same compassion and understanding you would extend to a loved one.

4. **Seek Support and Connections**
    - Build a supportive network of friends, family members, or professionals who understand and accept your neurodiversity.
    - Join online communities or support groups to connect with others who share similar experiences.
    - Surround yourself with individuals who celebrate your strengths and provide encouragement.

5. **Reframe Challenges as Opportunities**

• Instead of viewing ADHD symptoms as deficits, reframe them as opportunities for growth and personal development.

- For example, embrace your ability to adapt quickly and think creatively in challenging situations.
- Celebrate small victories and milestones along your journey.

6. **Advocate for Yourself**

- Develop the confidence to communicate your needs and advocate for accommodations or support when necessary.
- Educate others about ADHD and your unique strengths and challenges.
- Be proactive in creating an environment that allows you to

thrive and reach your full potential.

Building self-awareness and self-acceptance is an ongoing process, but it is a crucial step towards embracing your neurodiversity and living a fulfilling life with ADHD. Remember, your unique perspectives and abilities are valuable assets, and by cultivating selfacceptance, you can unlock your true potential and contribute to a more inclusive and understanding world.

Recognizing Your Strengths and Challenges

Attention Deficit Hyperactivity Disorder (ADHD) is a neurological condition that presents both unique strengths and challenges. Recognizing and understanding these aspects of your ADHD is a crucial step towards self-awareness, self-acceptance, and ultimately, thriving in various aspects of your life. Here's a closer look at how you can identify and leverage your strengths while addressing your challenges:

Recognizing Your Strengths 1. **Creativity and Out-of-the-Box Thinking**

- Embrace your ability to think divergently and approach problems from unique angles.
- Harness your creativity in artistic pursuits, problem-solving, or innovative endeavors.

2. **Hyperfocus and Intense Passion**

- Leverage your ability to become deeply immersed and focused on tasks or activities that genuinely interest you.

- Channel this hyperfocus into productive endeavors, hobbies, or areas of personal growth.

3. **Adaptability and Resilience**
   - Celebrate your ability to adapt quickly to changing situations and bounce back from setbacks.
   - Develop strategies to leverage this resilience in both personal and professional contexts.

4. **High Energy and Enthusiasm**
   - Recognize the contagious energy and enthusiasm you bring to projects, teams, or social interactions.
   - Harness this energy to fuel your passions and inspire others around you.

Acknowledging Your Challenges 1. **Time Management and Organization**

- Identify areas where you struggle with time management, prioritization, and organization.
- Develop practical strategies, such as using planners, apps, or accountability partners, to improve these skills.

2. **Sustained Attention and Focus**

- Recognize situations or tasks that pose challenges for sustaining your attention and focus.
- Explore techniques like the Pomodoro method, breaks, or environmental modifications to enhance your focus.

3. **Impulsivity and Emotional Regulation**

    - Be aware of moments when impulsivity or emotional dysregulation may impact your decisions or relationships.
    - Practice mindfulness, deep breathing exercises, or seek support to develop better selfregulation skills.

4. **Procrastination and Task Initiation**

    - Identify patterns of procrastination or difficulty starting tasks that you find less stimulating.
    - Implement strategies like breaking tasks into smaller steps, using rewards, or seeking accountability partners.

Remember, recognizing your strengths and challenges is not about labeling yourself but about gaining self-awareness and embracing your unique neurodiversity. By understanding these aspects of your ADHD, you can develop personalized strategies to leverage your strengths and address your challenges effectively.

Collaboration with healthcare professionals, educators, or coaches who specialize in ADHD can provide valuable guidance and support as you navigate this journey. Celebrate your strengths, and don't be afraid to seek accommodations or support when needed – it's all part of embracing your neurodiversity and thriving with ADHD.

Cultivating a Growth Mindset

Embracing a growth mindset is a powerful tool for individuals with Attention Deficit Hyperactivity Disorder (ADHD) to navigate the challenges they face and unlock their full potential. A growth mindset is the belief that abilities and intelligence can be developed through dedication, effort, and a willingness to learn from setbacks. Here are some strategies to cultivate a growth mindset when living with ADHD:

1. **Reframe Challenges as Opportunities**
    - Instead of viewing ADHD-related challenges as insurmountable obstacles, reframe them as opportunities for growth and personal development.
    - Recognize that setbacks and failures are not permanent but

rather stepping stones to learning and improvement.

- Celebrate small victories and milestones along your journey, as they represent progress and growth.

2. **Embrace a Mindset of Curiosity**

    - Approach challenges with a curious mindset, seeking to understand the root causes and explore potential solutions.
    - Ask questions, seek feedback, and remain open to new perspectives and strategies.
    - Cultivate a willingness to learn and try new approaches, even if they feel uncomfortable initially.

3. **Practice Self-Compassion**

- Be kind and understanding towards yourself when facing difficulties or setbacks.
- Avoid self-criticism or harsh selfjudgment, as these can hinder growth and resilience.
- Treat yourself with the same compassion and encouragement you would offer a loved one or a friend.

4. **Seek Out Constructive Feedback**

- Actively seek out constructive feedback from trusted sources, such as mentors, coaches, or professionals.
- Use this feedback as an opportunity to identify areas for improvement and develop targeted strategies.

- Celebrate feedback as a valuable tool for growth, rather than perceiving it as criticism.

5. **Surround Yourself with a Supportive Network**
    - Build a network of supportive individuals who understand and embrace a growth mindset.
    - Share your goals, challenges, and successes with this network, and seek encouragement and accountability.
    - Celebrate each other's progress and learn from one another's experiences.
6. **Celebrate Effort and Progress**
    - Recognize that progress and growth are the result of consistent effort and perseverance.

- Celebrate the effort you put into developing new skills or strategies, regardless of the immediate outcome.
- Keep track of your progress and reflect on how far you've come, rather than focusing solely on the destination.

Cultivating a growth mindset is an ongoing journey that requires patience, self-compassion, and a willingness to embrace challenges as opportunities for growth. By adopting this mindset, individuals with ADHD can unlock their full potential, develop resilience, and achieve personal and professional success while embracing their unique neurodiversity.

Practicing Self-Compassion

Hyperactivity Disorder (ADHD) can be a rollercoaster ride filled with challenges, setbacks, and moments of self-doubt. In such instances, practicing self-compassion can be a powerful tool to help you navigate these difficulties with greater resilience, self-acceptance, and overall well-being. Here are some strategies to cultivate self-compassion as an individual with ADHD:

1. **Recognize and Validate Your Experiences**
   - Acknowledge the unique challenges and struggles that come with living with ADHD.
   - Instead of minimizing or dismissing your experiences, validate and honor them as real and valid.

- Remind yourself that your feelings and struggles are understandable and deserving of compassion.

2. **Embrace Self-Kindness**
    - Treat yourself with the same kindness, understanding, and patience that you would extend to a loved one or a dear friend.
    - Avoid harsh self-criticism or negative self-talk, as these can exacerbate feelings of inadequacy and low self-worth.
    - Use gentle, encouraging self-talk to uplift yourself during difficult moments.

3. **Practice Mindfulness and PresentMoment Awareness**
    - Cultivate the ability to be present in the current moment,

rather than dwelling on past mistakes or worrying about the future.

- Use mindfulness techniques, such as deep breathing exercises or meditation, to ground yourself in the present.
- Observe your thoughts and emotions with a non-judgmental attitude, acknowledging them without getting caught up in them.

4. **Recognize the Common Humanity**
    - Understand that the struggles and challenges you face are part of the shared human experience.
    - Remind yourself that everyone faces difficulties and setbacks, and you are not alone in your journey.

- Connect with others who have similar experiences, either through support groups or online communities, to foster a sense of belonging and understanding.

5. **Celebrate Your Strengths and Accomplishments**
    - Identify and acknowledge your unique strengths, talents, and accomplishments, no matter how small.
    - Celebrate your progress and efforts, rather than solely focusing on perceived shortcomings or failures.
    - Use positive self-talk to reinforce your strengths and abilities, counterbalancing any negative self-talk.

6. **Seek Support and Professional Help**

   - Recognize that practicing selfcompassion can be challenging, and it's okay to seek support from others.
   - Consider working with a therapist or counselor who can provide guidance and techniques for cultivating self-compassion.
   - Surround yourself with a supportive network of friends, family, or professionals who can offer encouragement and understanding.

Practicing self-compassion is an ongoing journey that requires patience, mindfulness, and a commitment to self-care. By embracing self-compassion, individuals with ADHD can develop greater resilience, self-acceptance, and overall well-being, enabling them to navigate the challenges of life with greater ease and kindness towards themselves.

Chapter 3: Mastering Mindfulness and Attention Management

Mastering Mindfulness and Attention Management for Individuals with ADHD

For individuals with Attention Deficit Hyperactivity Disorder (ADHD), mastering mindfulness and attention management can be a game-changer in navigating the challenges of daily life. By cultivating present-moment awareness and developing strategies to regulate attention, you can unlock your full potential and thrive in various aspects of your personal and professional endeavors. Here are some practical strategies to help you on this journey:

1. **Mindfulness Meditation**
    - Incorporate mindfulness meditation into your daily

routine, even if it's just for a few minutes a day.

- During meditation, focus on your breath or a specific anchor, such as a mantra or a calming visualization.
- When your mind wanders (which it inevitably will), gently bring your attention back to the present moment without judgment.

2. **Body Awareness Exercises**

- Engage in practices that cultivate body awareness, such as yoga, tai chi, or progressive muscle relaxation.
- By tuning into your physical sensations and breath, you can anchor yourself in the present moment and reduce mental distractions.

3. **Mindful Movement**

    - Incorporate mindful movement into your routine, such as walking meditations or mindful stretching.
    - Pay attention to the sensations in your body as you move, focusing on the present experience rather than getting caught up in thoughts or distractions.

4. **Environmental Modifications**

    - Optimize your environment to minimize distractions and promote focus.
    - Consider using noise-canceling headphones, minimizing clutter, or creating a dedicated workspace free from visual clutter or distractions.

5. **Attention Management Techniques**

- Explore techniques like the Pomodoro method, which involves alternating periods of focused work with short breaks.
- Use timers or apps to help you stay on track and prevent hyperfocus on a single task.
- Break larger tasks into smaller, manageable steps to maintain focus and motivation.

6. **Mindful Listening and Communication**

- Practice mindful listening during conversations, giving your full attention to the person speaking without mentally wandering or planning your response.
- When communicating, pause and take a breath before responding, allowing yourself to

be present and thoughtful in your responses.

7. **Self-Compassion and Non-Judgment**
    - Embrace a non-judgmental attitude towards yourself when your mind wanders or you struggle to maintain focus.
    - Practice self-compassion and recognize that cultivating mindfulness and attention management is an ongoing process that requires patience and kindness towards yourself.

Mastering mindfulness and attention management is a journey that requires consistent practice and a willingness to explore different techniques until you find what works best for you. By incorporating these strategies into your daily life, you can develop greater present-moment awareness, enhance your ability to focus, and ultimately unlock your full potential while navigating the unique challenges of ADHD.

The Power of Mindfulness for ADHD

Mindfulness, the practice of cultivating present-moment awareness and non-judgmental acceptance, can be a powerful tool for individuals with Attention Deficit Hyperactivity Disorder (ADHD). By training the mind to stay focused on the present and letting go of distractions, mindfulness can help mitigate the challenges associated with ADHD and unlock a range of benefits. Here's a closer look at how mindfulness can positively impact individuals with ADHD:

1. **Improved Attention and Focus**
    - Mindfulness practices, such as meditation and body scans, train the mind to stay anchored in the present moment, reducing the tendency to get caught up in distracting thoughts or impulses.
    - Over time, this can enhance the ability to sustain attention and focus, which can be particularly beneficial for individuals with ADHD who struggle with concentration.
2. **Emotional Regulation**
    - Mindfulness promotes an awareness of emotional states without getting caught up in them, allowing individuals to respond more skillfully to intense emotions.

- By cultivating a non-judgmental attitude towards thoughts and feelings, mindfulness can help individuals with ADHD better manage impulsivity, emotional outbursts, and mood swings.

3. **Reduced Stress and Anxiety**

- The practice of mindfulness has been shown to reduce stress and anxiety levels by promoting relaxation and a more balanced perspective.
- For individuals with ADHD, who often experience heightened levels of stress and anxiety, mindfulness can provide a valuable coping mechanism and a sense of calm amidst the chaos.

4. **Improved Self-Awareness and SelfAcceptance**

- Mindfulness encourages individuals to observe their thoughts, emotions, and behaviors with a non-judgmental lens, fostering greater selfawareness and self-acceptance.
- By cultivating self-compassion, individuals with ADHD can learn

    to embrace their neurodiversity and focus on their strengths rather than perceived deficits.

5. **Enhanced Cognitive Flexibility**

    - Mindfulness practices can improve cognitive flexibility, the ability to shift perspectives and adapt to changing situations.
    - For individuals with ADHD, who may struggle with rigidity or difficulty transitioning between tasks, this can be a valuable skill

in navigating daily life and professional demands.

6. **Better Sleep and Overall Well-being**
   - By reducing stress and promoting relaxation, mindfulness can contribute to improved sleep quality and overall well-being.
   - For individuals with ADHD, who often experience sleep difficulties and related challenges, mindfulness can be a natural and effective way to cultivate a sense of calm and balance.

Incorporating mindfulness practices into daily life can be a transformative experience for individuals with ADHD. Whether through formal meditation practices, mindful movement, or simply cultivating present-moment awareness throughout the day, mindfulness offers a powerful tool for managing the unique challenges of ADHD and unlocking greater mental clarity, emotional resilience, and overall well-being.

Meditation and Mindfulness Practices

For individuals with Attention Deficit Hyperactivity Disorder (ADHD), incorporating meditation and mindfulness practices into their daily routine can be a powerful tool for managing symptoms, improving focus, and enhancing overall well-being. While it may seem counterintuitive at first, as these practices require sustained attention, with time and practice, they can help cultivate greater present-moment awareness and concentration. Here are some effective meditation and mindfulness practices for individuals with ADHD:

1. **Breath Awareness Meditation**
   - Begin by finding a comfortable seated position and gently closing your eyes.
   - Bring your attention to your natural breath, noticing the sensation of air moving in and out of your nostrils or the rise and fall of your abdomen.
   - When your mind wanders (which it inevitably will), gently redirect your focus back to your breath without judgment.
   - Start with short sessions of 5-10 minutes and gradually increase the duration as you build your mindfulness muscle.

2. **Body Scan Meditation**

- Lie down or sit comfortably and bring your attention to different parts of your body, one at a time.
- Notice any sensations, such as tension, relaxation, or tingling, without trying to change or judge them.

- Slowly scan through your entire body, cultivating a nonjudgmental awareness of physical sensations.
    - This practice can help ground individuals with ADHD in the present moment and reduce mental restlessness.

3. **Walking Meditation**

- Find a quiet space where you can walk slowly back and forth, indoors or outdoors.
- Bring your attention to the physical sensations of walking, such as the movement of your feet, the weight shifting from one foot to the other, and the gentle sway of your arms.
- When your mind wanders, gently redirect your focus to the physical sensations of walking.

- This practice can be particularly helpful for individuals with ADHD who find it challenging to sit still for extended periods.

4. **Mindful Listening**

- Find a quiet space and focus your attention on the sounds around you, near and far.
- Notice each sound without judging or labeling it, simply allowing it to rise and fall in your awareness.
- When your mind wanders, gently bring your attention back to the present moment and the sounds you can hear.
- This practice can help cultivate present-moment awareness and improve active listening skills.

-

5. **Mindful Movement**

Engage in gentle movement practices, such as yoga, tai chi, or mindful stretching.

- As you move, bring your attention to the sensations in your body, the rhythm of your breath, and the present moment experience.
- When your mind wanders, gently redirect your focus back to the physical sensations and movements.
- Mindful movement can help individuals with ADHD channel their energy and cultivate greater body awareness.

Remember, mindfulness and meditation practices are skills that require regular practice and patience. It's essential to approach these practices with self-compassion and avoid judgment or frustration if your mind wanders frequently. Over time, with consistent effort, these practices can help individuals with ADHD develop greater present-moment awareness, focus, and overall wellbeing.

Strategies for Sustained Focus and Concentration

Maintaining sustained focus and concentration can be a significant challenge for individuals with Attention Deficit Hyperactivity Disorder (ADHD). However, by implementing effective strategies and techniques, you can improve your ability to stay on task and enhance your productivity. Here are some practical strategies to help you cultivate sustained focus and concentration:

1. **The Pomodoro Technique**
   - This time-management method involves breaking work into intervals (traditionally 25 minutes) separated by short breaks.
   - Set a timer for the work interval and focus solely on the task at hand until the timer goes off.
   - Take a 5-minute break before starting the next work interval.
   - The short breaks help reset your focus and prevent mental fatigue or burnout.
2. **Eliminate Distractions**
   - Identify and remove potential distractions from your environment, such as social media notifications, background noise, or clutter.

- Use noise-canceling headphones or earplugs to block out auditory distractions.
- Consider using website blockers or apps that limit access to distracting websites or apps during designated work periods.

3. **Break Tasks into Smaller Steps**
    - Breaking larger tasks into smaller, manageable steps can make them feel less overwhelming and easier to focus on.
    - Create a checklist or visual representation of the steps involved, and tackle them one at a time.
    - Celebrate small wins as you complete each step, which can provide motivation and a sense of accomplishment.

4. **Use Visual Aids and Reminders**

    - Utilize visual aids, such as sticky notes, whiteboards, or digital reminders, to keep your goals and tasks visible.
    - Place these reminders in strategic locations where you'll see them frequently, helping to refocus your attention when it wanders.

5. **Practice Mindfulness and Meditation**

- Incorporating mindfulness practices, such as deep breathing exercises or short meditations, can help calm the mind and enhance presentmoment awareness.
- Even a few minutes of mindfulness practice before starting a task can improve your ability to sustain focus.

6. **Engage in Physical Activity**
    - Regular physical activity can help improve focus and concentration by increasing blood flow and releasing endorphins.
    - Incorporate short exercise breaks, such as walking or stretching, into your daily routine to re-energize and refocus.
7. **Experiment with Different Work Environments**
    - Some individuals with ADHD may find that certain environments, such as quiet spaces or background noise, better support their focus and concentration.
    - Experiment with different settings and find what works best for you, whether it's

working in a library, a coffee shop, or at home with instrumental music playing.

Remember, everyone's experience with ADHD is unique, and what works for one person may not be as effective for another. Be patient and open to trying different strategies until you find the combination that helps you maintain sustained focus and concentration. Celebrating small wins and practicing self-compassion throughout the process can also help you stay motivated and resilient.

Chapter 4: Optimizing Your Work Environment

Optimizing Your Work Environment for Individuals with ADHD

Creating an optimal work environment can significantly impact focus, productivity, and overall well-being for individuals with Attention Deficit Hyperactivity Disorder (ADHD). By tailoring your workspace to your unique needs and preferences, you can minimize distractions, enhance concentration, and foster a sense of calm and organization. Here are some strategies to help you optimize your work environment:

1. **Minimize Visual Clutter**
    - Reduce visual distractions by keeping your workspace organized and clutter-free.

- Use storage solutions, such as filing cabinets or shelves, to keep items out of sight and create a clean, streamlined space.
- Consider minimalist decor or adding plants to create a calming, natural environment.

2. **Control Auditory Distractions**

- Noise and auditory distractions can significantly impact concentration for individuals with ADHD.
- Use noise-canceling headphones or earplugs to block out external sounds.
- Experiment with different types of background noise, such as white noise, nature sounds, or instrumental music, to find what helps you stay focused.

3. **Optimize Lighting**

- Proper lighting can improve focus, reduce eye strain, and create a more inviting work environment.
- Maximize natural light by positioning your workspace near windows or using adjustable lamps.
- Avoid harsh, fluorescent lighting, which can be distracting and cause eye fatigue.

4. **Incorporate Movement**

- Individuals with ADHD often benefit from opportunities for movement and physical activity.
- Consider using a standing desk or exercise ball to encourage movement and prevent restlessness.

- Take regular breaks to stretch, walk around, or engage in brief physical activities to re-energize and refocus.

5. **Personalize Your Space**
    - Create a work environment that reflects your personality and interests.
    - Display inspirational quotes, artwork, or personal mementos that bring you joy and motivation.
    - Incorporate elements that stimulate your senses, such as aromatherapy or calming background music, to create a multisensory experience.

6. **Establish Boundaries**
    - If you work from home or share a workspace, establish clear

boundaries to minimize distractions and interruptions.

- Communicate your needs to family members, roommates, or colleagues, and set designated "focus times" when you should not be disturbed.
- Consider using visual cues, such as a "do not disturb" sign or noise-canceling headphones, to reinforce these boundaries.

7. **Experiment and Adapt**

- Remember that optimizing your work environment is an ongoing process, and what works best may change over time or depending on the task at hand.
- Be open to experimenting with different setups, organizational systems, or environmental modifications until you find the

combination that maximizes your focus and productivity.

By creating an environment that caters to your unique needs and preferences, you can minimize distractions, enhance concentration, and cultivate a productive and enjoyable work experience. Regularly reassessing and adjusting your workspace can also help you adapt to changing circumstances and maintain a supportive, focused environment.

Creating a Productive and Supportive Workspace

For individuals with Attention Deficit Hyperactivity Disorder (ADHD), having a workspace that is tailored to their specific needs can make a significant difference in productivity, focus, and overall well-being. By creating an environment that minimizes distractions, fosters concentration, and provides a sense of calm and organization, you can optimize your ability to stay on task and achieve your goals. Here are some strategies for creating a productive and supportive workspace:

1. **Minimize Visual Clutter**
    - Declutter your workspace by removing unnecessary items and organizing essentials.
    - Use storage solutions like file cabinets, shelves, or bins to keep items out of sight.
    - Consider minimalist decor or adding plants for a calming, natural environment.

2. **Control Auditory Distractions**
   - Invest in noise-canceling headphones or earplugs to block out external sounds.
   - Experiment with different types of background noise, such as white noise, nature sounds, or instrumental music, to find what helps you concentrate.
3. **Optimize Lighting**
   - Maximize natural light by positioning your workspace near windows or using adjustable lamps.
   - Avoid harsh, fluorescent lighting, which can be distracting and cause eye strain.
4. **Incorporate Movement**
   - Use a standing desk, exercise ball, or take regular breaks to

move around and prevent restlessness.

- Engage in brief physical activities or stretches to re-energize and refocus.

5. **Personalize Your Space**

- Display inspirational quotes, artwork, or personal mementos that bring you joy and motivation.
- Incorporate elements that stimulate your senses, such as aromatherapy or calming background music.

6. **Establish Boundaries**
   - Set designated "focus times" when you should not be disturbed, and communicate your needs to others.
   - Use visual cues like a "do not disturb" sign or noise-canceling headphones to reinforce boundaries.
7. **Implement Organizational Systems**
   - Use calendars, planners, or digital tools to stay organized

and manage your time effectively.

- Establish routines and create checklists or visual aids to help you stay on track.

8. **Foster a Positive Mindset**

    - Surround yourself with motivational reminders, affirmations, or inspiring quotes to cultivate a growth mindset.
    - Celebrate small wins and practice self-compassion to maintain a positive and supportive attitude.

9. **Experiment and Adapt**

    - Be open to trying different setups, organizational systems, or environmental modifications to find the combination that works best for you.

- Regularly reassess and adjust your workspace to adapt to changing circumstances or task requirements.

By creating a workspace that caters to your unique needs and preferences, you can minimize distractions, enhance concentration, and cultivate a productive and enjoyable work environment. Remember, optimizing your workspace is an ongoing process, and what works best may change over time. Be patient, experiment, and celebrate the small victories along the way.

Minimizing Distractions and Sensory Overload

For individuals with Attention Deficit Hyperactivity Disorder (ADHD), distractions and sensory overload can significantly impact focus, productivity, and overall well-being. Sensory input, whether visual, auditory, or tactile, can be overwhelming and lead to feelings of overwhelm or overstimulation. By implementing strategies to minimize distractions and manage sensory input, you can create a more conducive environment for concentration and task completion. Here are some effective strategies to consider:

1. **Visual Distractions**

    - Declutter your workspace by removing unnecessary items and organizing essentials neatly.
    - Use storage solutions like file cabinets, shelves, or bins to keep items out of sight and reduce visual clutter.

- Consider minimalist decor or adding plants for a calming, natural environment.

2. **Auditory Distractions**
    - Invest in high-quality noisecanceling headphones or earplugs to block out external sounds.
    - Experiment with different types of background noise, such as white noise, nature sounds, or instrumental music, to find what helps you concentrate.
    - If working in a shared space, communicate your need for a quieter environment with others.
3. **Tactile and Sensory Stimulation**
    - Identify and minimize sources of tactile distractions, such as tight

clothing, uncomfortable seating, or unnecessary fidgeting.

- Consider using fidget toys or stress balls to provide a healthy outlet for restless energy or sensory input.
- Incorporate sensory-friendly elements, such as weighted blankets, calming scents, or textured surfaces, to create a soothing environment.

4. **Lighting and Visual Stimuli**

- Optimize lighting by maximizing natural light or using adjustable lamps to reduce eye strain and visual fatigue.
- Avoid harsh, fluorescent lighting or bright, flashing screens that can be overstimulating.

- Use blue light filters or adjust screen brightness to minimize

- visual stimulation from digital devices.

5. **Create a Dedicated Work Zone**
   - Designate a specific area or room as your dedicated workspace, free from distractions and sensory overload.
   - Establish boundaries and communicate your need for focused time to others in your household or workspace.
   - Use visual cues like a "do not disturb" sign or noise-canceling headphones to reinforce your boundaries.

6. **Implement Routines and Breaks**
   - Establish routines and schedules that allow for focused work

periods followed by scheduled breaks.

During breaks, engage in activities that provide sensory relief, such as stretching, deep breathing exercises, or short walks.

- Use timers or apps to help you stay on track and prevent hyperfocus or burnout.

7. **Seek Professional Support**

- If sensory overload or distractions persist despite your efforts, consider seeking support from an occupational therapist or mental health professional who specializes in ADHD.
- They can provide personalized strategies and accommodations to help you manage sensory

- input and distractions more effectively.

Remember, minimizing distractions and sensory overload is an ongoing process that may require experimentation and adjustments. Be patient with yourself, and celebrate the small victories along the way. By creating an environment that supports your unique needs, you can improve your focus, productivity, and overall well-being.

Leveraging Technology and Tools

In today's digital age, technology and tools can be powerful allies for individuals with Attention Deficit Hyperactivity Disorder (ADHD). By leveraging the right applications, devices, and software, you can enhance your ability to stay organized, manage time effectively, and minimize distractions. Here are some helpful technology and tools to consider:

1. **Productivity and Task Management Apps**

   Apps like Trello, Asana, or Todoist can help you break down larger tasks into manageable steps, set reminders, and track progress.

   - These tools often feature visual cues, customizable boards, and collaboration features, making them ideal for individuals with ADHD.

2. **Time Management and Focus Apps**

   - Apps like Forest, Focus Keeper, or the Pomodoro Technique can help you stay on task by blocking distracting websites or apps for set periods.

-

- They often incorporate gamification elements or reward systems to incentivize focused work sessions.

3. **Note-Taking and Organization Apps**

- Apps like Evernote, OneNote, or Google Keep can help you capture thoughts, ideas, and todo lists in one centralized location.

  - Many of these apps offer features like voice-to-text transcription, image recognition, and cloud synchronization across devices.

4. **Noise-Canceling Headphones or Earbuds**

- Investing in high-quality noisecanceling headphones or earbuds can help minimize auditory distractions and create a more focused environment.
- Look for models with ambient noise control or customizable sound settings to find the optimal level of noise reduction.

•

5. **Smart Home Devices and Assistants**

Virtual assistants like Amazon's Alexa, Google Assistant, or Apple's Siri can help you stay organized and on schedule with voice commands and reminders.

- Smart home devices like smart lights, thermostats, or speakers can create a customized environment conducive to focus and productivity.

6. **Fidget Toys and Sensory Tools**

- Fidget toys, stress balls, or other sensory tools can provide a healthy outlet for restless energy or sensory input.
- Look for fidget cubes, spinning rings, or textured objects that can be manipulated discreetly while working or studying.

•

7. **Ergonomic Workstations**

Investing in an ergonomic workstation, such as a standing desk, adjustable monitor arm, or ergonomic chair, can help promote better posture, reduce fatigue, and improve focus.

• Experiment with different setups to find the most comfortable and productive configuration.

8. **Biofeedback and Neurofeedback Devices**

- Biofeedback devices like heart rate monitors or neurofeedback systems can help you understand and regulate your physiological responses to stress or distractions.
- While these tools may require professional guidance, they can provide

- valuable insights and strategies for self-regulation.

Remember, the effectiveness of these tools and technologies may vary from person to person, and it's essential to explore and find the combination that works best for your unique needs and preferences. Don't be afraid to experiment and seek guidance from professionals or support groups if needed. By leveraging the right technology and tools, you can create an environment that supports your focus, productivity, and overall wellbeing.

Chapter 5: Time Management and Prioritization

Time Management and Prioritization Strategies for Individuals with ADHD

Effective time management and prioritization can be challenging for individuals with Attention Deficit Hyperactivity Disorder (ADHD), but implementing the right strategies can help you stay organized, focused, and productive. By developing a system that works with your unique strengths and challenges, you can better manage your time, prioritize tasks, and achieve your goals. Here are some practical strategies to consider:

1. **Use a Time Management System**
    - Explore different time management systems, such as

the Pomodoro Technique, time blocking, or the Eisenhower Matrix, to find the one that resonates with you.

- Break larger tasks into smaller, manageable steps and allocate specific time blocks for focused work.
- Use timers or apps to help you stay on track and prevent hyperfocus or procrastination.

2. **Prioritize and Categorize Tasks**
   - Create a comprehensive task list and categorize tasks based on urgency, importance, or other relevant criteria.
   - Use visual cues, such as colorcoding or symbols, to quickly identify high-priority tasks.

- Consider the "Ivy Lee Method," which involves prioritizing the day's tasks and focusing solely on the most important one until completion.

3. **Schedule Important Tasks First**
    - Plan your day by scheduling the most important or challenging tasks during your peak productivity hours.
    - Tackle these tasks when your energy and focus levels are highest, and save less demanding tasks for later in the day.
4. **Minimize Distractions and Multitasking**
    - Identify and eliminate potential distractions, such as social media

notifications or background noise.

- Practice single-tasking by focusing on one task at a time until completion, rather than attempting to juggle multiple tasks simultaneously.

5. **Build in Breaks and Rewards**

- Incorporate regular breaks into your schedule to prevent burnout and maintain focus.
- Use these breaks to engage in physical activity, mindfulness practices, or enjoyable activities that help you recharge.
- Celebrate small wins and reward yourself for completing tasks or reaching milestones.

6. **Leverage Technology and Tools**

- Utilize productivity apps, calendars, reminders, and other digital tools to help you stay organized and on track.
- Experiment with different apps or devices to find the ones that best suit your needs and preferences.

7. **Seek Support and Accountability**

- Consider working with an accountability partner, coach, or support group to stay motivated and on track.
- Share your goals, priorities, and challenges with trusted individuals who can provide encouragement and accountability.

8. **Practice Self-Reflection and Adjustment**

   - Regularly evaluate your time management and prioritization strategies, and make adjustments as needed.
   - Be flexible and open to trying new approaches or modifying existing systems to better align with your changing needs or circumstances.

Remember, effective time management and prioritization are ongoing processes that require consistent effort and selfawareness. Be patient with yourself, celebrate small victories, and don't be afraid to seek support when needed. By implementing strategies that work with your unique strengths and challenges, you can better manage your time, stay focused, and achieve your goals.

Understanding Your Energy Cycles

For individuals with Attention Deficit Hyperactivity Disorder (ADHD), understanding and working with your natural energy cycles can be a gamechanger in terms of productivity and focus. By identifying your peak performance periods and aligning your tasks accordingly, you can maximize your efficiency and minimize the impact of ADHD-related challenges. Here are some strategies to help you understand and leverage your energy cycles:

1. **Track Your Energy Levels**
    - Use a journal, app, or simple note-taking system to record your energy levels throughout the day.

- Note when you feel most alert, focused, and productive, as well as when you experience dips in energy or concentration.
- Look for patterns over a few weeks to identify your natural highs and lows.

2. **Identify Your Chronotype**
    - Determine whether you are a morning person (lark), night owl (wolf), or somewhere in between.
    - Your chronotype can influence your energy levels and peak performance times throughout the day.
    - Adjust your schedule and tasks to align with your natural rhythms when possible.

3. **Schedule Demanding Tasks During Peak Times**

    - Once you've identified your most productive periods, schedule your most challenging or mentally demanding tasks during these times.
    - Tackle projects that require sustained focus, critical thinking, or creativity when your energy levels are highest.

4. **Plan Less Demanding Tasks for Low Energy Times**

    - During your natural energy dips, schedule less mentally taxing tasks or activities that require less intense focus.
    - Use these times for administrative tasks, light reading, or simple chores that

don't require as much mental effort.

5. **Build in Breaks and Transitions**
    - Incorporate regular breaks and transition periods between tasks or energy cycles.
    - Use these breaks to engage in physical activity, mindfulness practices, or enjoyable activities that help you recharge and reset.
6. **Experiment with Productivity Techniques**
    - Try techniques like the Pomodoro Method, time blocking, or the "Body Double" approach to maximize your focus during peak periods.
    - Adjust and modify these techniques to find what works

best for your unique energy patterns and preferences.

7. **Optimize Your Environment**
   - Create an environment that supports your productivity and energy levels.
   - Adjust lighting, temperature, noise levels, and workspace organization to promote focus during peak times and relaxation during low energy periods.
8. **Be Flexible and Adaptable**
   - Remember that your energy cycles may fluctuate due to factors like stress, sleep quality, or changes in routine.
   - Be prepared to adjust your schedule and approach as needed, and don't be too rigid in your expectations.

By understanding and working with your natural energy cycles, you can maximize your productivity and minimize the impact of ADHD-related challenges. Be patient with yourself, and celebrate small victories along the way. With time and practice, you'll develop a system that harnesses your unique strengths and supports your overall well-being.

Effective Planning and Scheduling Techniques

For individuals with Attention Deficit Hyperactivity Disorder (ADHD), effective planning and scheduling can be a significant challenge. However, implementing the right techniques can help you stay organized, manage your time effectively, and increase productivity. Here are some practical planning and scheduling strategies to consider:

1. **Use a Physical or Digital Planner**
    - Choose a planner or calendar system that works best for you, whether it's a paper planner, a digital app, or a combination of both.
    - Write down all your tasks, appointments, and deadlines in one centralized location to avoid forgetting important dates or commitments.
2. **Break Tasks into Smaller Steps**
    - Break larger projects or tasks into smaller, manageable steps or subtasks.
    - This can make overwhelming tasks feel more approachable

and help you maintain focus and motivation.

3. **Prioritize Tasks**

    - Use a prioritization system, such as the Eisenhower Matrix or the ABCDE method, to categorize tasks based on urgency and importance.
    - Focus on high-priority tasks first, and schedule them during your peak productivity hours.

4. **Implement Time Blocking**

- Divide your day into dedicated time blocks for specific tasks or activities.
    - This can help you stay focused and prevent task-switching or distractions.

5. **Use Visual Cues and Reminders**
    - Incorporate visual cues, such as color-coding, sticky notes, or digital reminders, to help you stay on track and remember important tasks or deadlines.

6. **Schedule Buffer Time**

- Account for potential distractions, unexpected events, or task underestimation by scheduling buffer time between appointments or tasks.
- This can help reduce stress and prevent feelings of overwhelm.

-

7. **Batch Similar Tasks Together**

Group similar tasks or activities together, such as answering emails, making phone calls, or running errands.

- This can help you maintain focus and momentum, and reduce the time spent switching between different types of tasks.

8. **Build in Breaks and Rewards**

- Schedule regular breaks throughout the day to prevent burnout and maintain focus.
- Use these breaks to engage in physical activity, mindfulness practices, or enjoyable activities that help you recharge.

- Celebrate small wins and reward yourself for completing tasks or reaching milestones.

9. **Seek Accountability and Support**
Consider working with an accountability partner, coach, or support group to stay motivated and on track.

    - Share your goals, plans, and challenges with trusted individuals who can provide encouragement and accountability.

10. **Regularly Review and Adjust**

- Review your planning and scheduling system regularly, and make adjustments as needed.
- Be flexible and open to trying new approaches or modifying existing strategies to better align with your changing needs or circumstances.

- Remember, effective planning and scheduling are ongoing processes that require consistency and selfawareness. Be patient with yourself, celebrate small victories, and don't be afraid to seek support when needed. By implementing strategies that work with your unique strengths and challenges, you can better manage your time, increase productivity, and achieve your goals.

Prioritizing Tasks and Managing Deadlines

For individuals with Attention Deficit Hyperactivity Disorder (ADHD), prioritizing tasks and managing deadlines can be a significant challenge. However, implementing the right strategies can help you stay organized, focused, and productive, even when faced with multiple competing demands. Here are some effective techniques to consider:

1. **Use a Priority Matrix**
   - Implement a priority matrix, such as the Eisenhower Matrix

     or the ABCDE method, to categorize tasks based on urgency and importance.
   - Focus on high-priority tasks first, and schedule them during your peak productivity hours.
2. **Break Down Large Tasks**
   - Break larger projects or tasks into smaller, manageable steps or subtasks.
   - This can make overwhelming tasks feel more approachable and help you maintain focus and motivation.

3. **Set Realistic Deadlines**

- When setting deadlines, be realistic about the time and effort required for each task.
- Account for potential distractions, unexpected events, or task underestimation by building in buffer time.

4. **Use Visual Cues and Reminders**

- Incorporate visual cues, such as color-coding, sticky notes, or digital reminders, to help you stay on track and remember important deadlines.
- Use a physical or digital calendar to keep track of due dates and milestones.

5. **Eliminate Distractions**

   - Identify and eliminate potential distractions, such as social media notifications or background noise, during focused work sessions.
   - Use tools like website blockers, noise-canceling headphones, or designated "focus zones" to minimize interruptions.

6. **Implement Time Blocking**

   - Divide your day into dedicated time blocks for specific tasks or activities.
   - This can help you stay focused and prevent task-switching or distractions.

7. **Build in Accountability**

   - Consider working with an accountability partner, coach, or support group to stay motivated and on track.

- Share your goals, priorities, and deadlines with trusted individuals who can provide encouragement and accountability.

8. **Practice Time Management Techniques**

    - Explore time management techniques like the Pomodoro Method, which involves working in focused intervals with built-in breaks.
    - Adjust and modify these techniques to find what works best for your unique needs and preferences.

9. **Celebrate Small Wins**

- Recognize and celebrate small victories along the way, such as completing a subtask or meeting a milestone.
- This can help maintain motivation and prevent feelings of overwhelm.

10. **Regularly Review and Adjust**

- Review your prioritization and deadline management strategies regularly, and make adjustments as needed.

- Be flexible and open to trying new approaches or modifying existing strategies to better align with your changing needs or circumstances.

Remember, prioritizing tasks and managing deadlines are ongoing processes that require consistency and self-awareness. Be patient with yourself, and don't be afraid to seek support when needed. By implementing strategies that work with your unique strengths and challenges, you can better manage your time, increase productivity, and achieve your goals while maintaining a healthy work-life balance.

Chapter 6: Communication and Interpersonal Dynamics

Communication and Interpersonal Dynamics for Individuals with ADHD

Effective communication and navigating interpersonal dynamics can be challenging for individuals with Attention Deficit Hyperactivity Disorder (ADHD). However, understanding your unique strengths and challenges, and implementing the right strategies, can help you foster better relationships and improve your overall communication skills. Here are some tips to consider:

1. **Active Listening**

    - Practice active listening techniques, such as maintaining eye contact, nodding, and repeating key points to ensure

-

  you fully understand the other person's perspective.

  Avoid interrupting or jumping ahead, which can be common tendencies for individuals with ADHD.

2. **Clear and Concise Communication**
   - Express your thoughts and ideas in a clear and concise manner, focusing on the most important points.
   - Break down complex information into smaller, more digestible chunks to aid comprehension and retention.
3. **Seek Clarification**
   - Don't be afraid to ask for clarification or additional explanation if you're unsure about something.

- Rephrase and repeat important information to ensure you've understood correctly.

4. **Manage Impulsivity**
   - Be mindful of impulsive reactions or remarks, which can strain relationships or create misunderstandings.
   - Take a moment to pause and collect your thoughts before responding, especially in emotionally charged situations.

5. **Establish Boundaries**
   - Communicate your boundaries and needs clearly, whether it's related to personal space, interruptions, or specific accommodations.
   - Respect the boundaries of others as well, and be open to

- finding mutually agreeable solutions.

6. **Leverage Strengths**

   Identify and leverage your unique strengths, such as creativity, problem-solving abilities, or a talent for thinking outside the box.

   • Share your insights and perspectives in a constructive and respectful manner.

7. **Seek Feedback**

   - Actively seek feedback from trusted individuals on your communication style and interpersonal interactions.
   - Be open to constructive criticism and use it as an opportunity for growth and improvement.

8. **Practice Mindfulness**

- Engage in mindfulness practices, such as deep breathing exercises or meditation, to help you stay present and focused during conversations.
- This can also help you manage emotional reactions and impulsivity.

9. **Build a Support System**

- Surround yourself with a supportive network of individuals who understand and accept you, including friends, family, or a support group.
- Don't be afraid to seek professional help, such as counseling or coaching, if needed.

-

10. **Continuous Learning**

    - Communication and interpersonal skills are ongoing processes that require continuous learning and practice.

      Be patient with yourself, celebrate small victories, and remain open to trying new techniques or strategies.

Remember, effective communication and navigating interpersonal dynamics are essential for building and maintaining healthy relationships, both personal and professional. By understanding your unique strengths and challenges, and implementing strategies that work for you, you can improve your communication skills and foster more meaningful connections with others.

Building Strong Relationships and Rapport

For individuals with Attention Deficit Hyperactivity Disorder (ADHD), building and maintaining strong relationships can be a significant challenge. However, by understanding your unique strengths and implementing effective strategies, you can foster meaningful connections and build rapport with others. Here are some tips to consider:

1. **Practice Active Listening**
    - Actively listen to others without interrupting or getting distracted.
    - Maintain eye contact, nod, and repeat key points to show you're engaged and understand their perspective.

-

2. **Show Genuine Interest**
    - Ask questions and show genuine interest in the other person's thoughts, feelings, and experiences.
    - Remember and follow up on important details to

demonstrate that you value the relationship.

3. **Be Reliable and Accountable**
    - Follow through on commitments and obligations, even if it means setting reminders or asking for help.
    - Acknowledge mistakes or missed deadlines, and take responsibility for your actions.
4. **Offer Support and Encouragement**
    - Provide emotional support and encouragement to those in your life, whether it's celebrating their successes or offering a listening ear during challenging times.
5. **Share Your Authentic Self**

- Be open and honest about your experiences with ADHD, and

share your unique perspectives and insights.

- Embrace your strengths and positive qualities, and let them shine through in your interactions.

6. **Practice Empathy and Patience**
    - Make an effort to understand and validate the feelings and experiences of others, even if they differ from your own.
    - Be patient and avoid judgment, as building trust and rapport takes time.

7. **Manage Impulsivity and Distractibility**
    - Be mindful of impulsive reactions or tendencies that could strain relationships, such as interrupting or changing topics abruptly.

- Implement strategies like taking a pause before responding or minimizing external distractions during conversations.

8. **Seek Feedback and Improve**
    - Actively seek feedback from trusted individuals on your interpersonal skills and relationship-building efforts.
    - Use this feedback as an opportunity for growth and improvement, and be open to trying new techniques or strategies.
9. **Build a Support System**
    - Surround yourself with a supportive network of individuals who understand and accept you, including friends, family, or a support group.

- Seek professional help, such as counseling or coaching, if needed, to develop stronger interpersonal skills.

10. **Continuous Learning and Practice**
    - Building strong relationships and rapport is an ongoing process that requires continuous learning and practice.
    - Be patient with yourself, celebrate small victories, and remain open to trying new approaches.

Remember, strong relationships and rapport are essential for personal and professional growth, as well as overall well-being. By understanding your unique strengths and challenges, and implementing strategies that work for you, you can foster more meaningful connections and build a supportive network of individuals who understand and appreciate you.

Navigating Social Cues and Boundaries

For individuals with Attention Deficit Hyperactivity Disorder (ADHD), navigating social cues and boundaries can be a significant challenge. However, by developing selfawareness and implementing effective strategies, you can improve your ability to read and respond to social situations appropriately. Here are some tips to consider:

1. **Learn to Recognize Social Cues**
   - Pay attention to nonverbal cues, such as body language, facial expressions, and tone of voice.
   - Notice when someone seems disinterested, uncomfortable, or

wants to change the subject or end a conversation.

2. **Practice Mindfulness and SelfAwareness**
    - Engage in mindfulness practices, such as deep breathing exercises or meditation, to help you stay present and focused during social interactions.
    - Develop self-awareness by reflecting on your own behaviors and how they might be perceived by others.
3. **Seek Feedback and Insight**
    - Ask trusted friends or family members for honest feedback on your social skills and ability to read cues.

- Be open to constructive criticism and use it as an opportunity for growth and improvement.

4. **Respect Personal Boundaries**
    - Learn to recognize and respect others' boundaries, whether it's personal space, topics of conversation, or physical touch.
    - Communicate your own boundaries clearly and assertively, without being confrontational.
5. **Manage Impulsivity and Interruptions**
    - Be mindful of your tendency to interrupt or speak impulsively, which can be perceived as rude or disrespectful.
    - Practice pausing before responding, and actively listen to others without interrupting.

6. **Learn from Mistakes**

   - If you inadvertently cross a boundary or miss a social cue, acknowledge it and apologize sincerely.
   - Use these experiences as learning opportunities to improve your social awareness and sensitivity.

7. **Build a Support System**

   - Surround yourself with understanding and supportive individuals who can provide guidance and feedback on social situations.
   - Consider joining a support group or seeking professional help, such as counseling or coaching, if needed.

8. **Educate Others**

- Share information about ADHD and its impact on social skills with those who are willing to learn and understand.
- This can help build empathy and create a more supportive environment.

9. **Practice in Low-Risk Situations**

- Start by practicing social skills and boundary-setting in low-risk situations, such as with close friends or family members.
- Gradually build confidence and experience before tackling more challenging social situations.

10. **Be Patient and Kind to Yourself**

- Navigating social cues and boundaries is an ongoing process that requires patience and selfcompassion.

- Celebrate small victories and recognize that progress may be gradual.

Remember, social skills and boundarysetting are essential for building and maintaining healthy relationships, both personal and professional. By developing self-awareness, seeking feedback, and implementing effective strategies, you can improve your ability to navigate social situations and foster more meaningful connections with others.

Resolving Conflicts and Misunderstandings

For individuals with Attention Deficit Hyperactivity Disorder (ADHD), conflicts and misunderstandings can arise due to various factors, such as impulsivity, difficulty with emotional regulation, or challenges in communication and social cues. However, by implementing effective strategies, you can learn to resolve conflicts and misunderstandings in a constructive and respectful manner. Here are some tips to consider:

1. **Practice Active Listening**
   - Make a conscious effort to listen attentively to the other person's perspective without interrupting or getting distracted.
   - Repeat back key points to ensure you have understood correctly and to show that you are engaged in the conversation.

2. **Manage Impulsivity and Emotional Regulation**
    - Be mindful of your tendency to react impulsively or become overwhelmed by strong emotions.
    - Take a break if needed, and practice calming techniques, such as deep breathing or mindfulness exercises, before continuing the conversation.
3. **Seek Clarification**
    - Don't be afraid to ask questions or seek clarification if you're unsure about something.
    - Rephrase or repeat important points to ensure there are no misunderstandings.

4. **Use "I" Statements**

- Express your thoughts and feelings using "I" statements, rather than accusatory or blaming language.
- For example, "I felt hurt when you said..." instead of "You hurt me by saying..."

5. **Find Common Ground**

- Look for areas of agreement or shared goals, even if you disagree on specific points.

  - Building on common ground can help foster a more collaborative and constructive approach to resolving the conflict.

6. **Suggest Compromises or Solutions**

- Be open to considering compromises or creative solutions that address the needs and concerns of both parties.
- Approach the situation with a problem-solving mindset, rather than a "win-lose" mentality.

7. **Apologize and Take Responsibility** •
   If you have contributed to the conflict or misunderstanding, take responsibility and offer a sincere apology.

- Be specific about what you're apologizing for and express a genuine desire to improve the situation.

8. **Seek External Support**

- If the conflict or misunderstanding persists, consider seeking the assistance of a neutral third party, such as a mediator, counselor, or trusted friend or family member.
- An outside perspective can often help identify areas of compromise or provide strategies for effective communication.

9. **Learn from the Experience**

- Reflect on the conflict or misunderstanding once it has been resolved, and identify areas for personal growth or improvement.

- Use these experiences as opportunities to develop better communication, emotional regulation, and conflict resolution skills.

10. **Practice Self-Compassion**

- Resolving conflicts and misunderstandings can be challenging, especially for individuals with ADHD.
- Be patient and kind to yourself, celebrate small victories, and remember that progress is an ongoing process.

Remember, conflicts and misunderstandings are a natural part of any relationship, but how we approach and resolve them can make a significant difference. By implementing effective strategies, practicing self-awareness, and seeking support when needed, you can learn to navigate conflicts and misunderstandings in a constructive and respectful manner, fostering stronger and more meaningful connections with others.

Printed by Libri Plureos GmbH in Hamburg,
Germany

9 781806 251049